# States
# FLORIDA

by Jason Kirchner

CAPSTONE PRESS
a capstone imprint

Next Page Books are published by Capstone Press,
1710 Roe Crest Drive, North Mankato, Minnesota 56003
www.mycapstone.com

**Library of Congress Cataloging-in-Publication Data**
Cataloging-in-publication information is on file with the Library of
Congress.
ISBN 978-1-5157-0395-2 (library binding)
ISBN 978-1-5157-0455-3 (paperback)
ISBN 978-1-5157-0507-9 (ebook PDF)

**Editorial Credits**
Jaclyn Jaycox, editor; Richard Korab and Katy LaVigne, designers;
Morgan Walters, media researcher; Laura Manthe, production specialist

**Photo Credits**
Alamy: Niday Picture Library, 25; Capstone Press: Angi Gahler, map
4, 7; CriaImages.com: Jay Robert Nash Collection, top 18; Dreamstime:
Scott Anderson, bottom 19, Valentin Armianu, 10; Getty Images:
Buyenlarge, 27, Stock Montage, 12; Library of Congress: Prints and
Photographs Division/Carl Van Vechten, top 19; National Archives &
Records Administration, middle 19; Newscom: HAHN-KHAYAT/KRT,
middle 18; One Mile Up, Inc., 22–23; Shutterstock: Artem Furman,
bottom right 21, Aspen Photo, bottom 24, Bertl123, 9, Beth Swanson,
bottom left 21, middle left 21, Caz Harris Photography, top right 21,
forestpath, top left 20, fstockfoto, bottom left 8, Greg Amptman, top
left 21, Jill Nightingale, bottom left 20, Joseph Sohm, 28, Kamira, 16,
lev radin, bottom 18, Lyndsey McCall, 11, MaIII Themd, top right 20,
mariakraynova, 7, Parnumas Na Phatthalung, top 24, Raffaella Calzoni,
bottom right 20, Ricardo Reitmeyer, bottom right 8, Richard Cavalleri,
5, Ruth Peterkin, 17, Sean Pavone, 6, Sherry Yates Young, 29, Steven
Frame, 13, 14, Stocked House Studio, 15, ventdusud, cover; Wikimedia:
Ralph Eleaser Whiteside Earl, 26, Wilson44691, middle right 21

All design elements by Shutterstock

Printed and bound in China.
0316/CA21600187
012016   009436F16

# TABLE OF CONTENTS

Want to take your research further? Ask your librarian if your school subscribes to PebbleGo Next. If so, when you see this helpful symbol 🖰 throughout the book, log onto www.pebblegonext.com for bonus downloads and information.

# LOCATION

Most of Florida is a peninsula. It is mainly surrounded by water. On the east is the Atlantic Ocean. On the west is the Gulf of Mexico, a part of the Atlantic Ocean. The northwestern part of Florida is called the Panhandle. It is a narrow strip of land that extends west. Tallahassee, the state capital, is in the Panhandle. Jacksonville, Miami, and Tampa are the state's biggest cities.

**PebbleGo Next Bonus!** To print and label your own map, go to www.pebblegonext.com and search keywords: **FL MAP**

The population of Miami is about 420,000.

# GEOGRAPHY

Florida has sandy beaches, swamps, and deep forests. Florida's coast is 1,350 miles (2,173 kilometers) long. Long barrier islands, or sandbars, lie offshore. The Florida Keys are found south of the mainland. They are a long string of islands. The Everglades in southern Florida is the biggest swamp in the United States. Central Florida is full of hills and valleys, with thousands of small lakes. Northern Florida is covered with forests and hills. Florida's highest point is Britton Hill in northern Florida. It is 345 feet (105 meters) tall.

**PebbleGo Next Bonus!**
**To watch a video about Cypress Slough, go to www.pebblegonext.com and search keywords:**
**FL VIDEO**

Orlando is located in central Florida and is home to many famous attractions.

The Everglades National Park is visited by about one million people each year.

Britton Hill

Apalachicola River

Ochlockonee River

NORTHERN HIGHLANDS

MARIANNA LOWLANDS

ATLANTIC OCEAN

St. Johns River

CENTRAL HIGHLANDS

COASTAL LOWLANDS

Suwannee River

Withlacoochee River

Kissimmee River

Gulf of Mexico

COASTAL LOWLANDS

Lake Okeechobee

SOUTHERN ZONE

**Legend**

▲ Highest Point

⬭ Lake

▨ National Parks and Monuments

〰 River

Everglades National Park

Biscayne National Park

Florida Keys

Scale

Miles
0    40    80    120

0   40   80   120   160
Kilometers

# WEATHER

In most of Florida, a cool, dry winter follows a warm, rainy summer. The average winter temperature is 59 degrees Fahrenheit (15 degrees Celsius). The average summer temperature is 81°F (27°C).

## Average High and Low Temperatures (Orlando, FL)

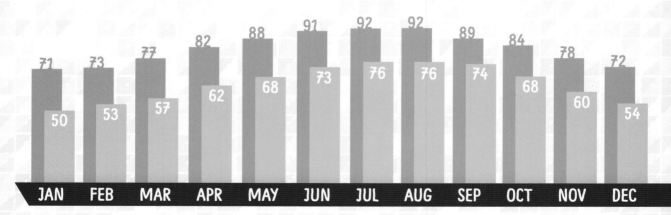

| | JAN | FEB | MAR | APR | MAY | JUN | JUL | AUG | SEP | OCT | NOV | DEC |
|---|---|---|---|---|---|---|---|---|---|---|---|---|
| High | 71 | 73 | 77 | 82 | 88 | 91 | 92 | 92 | 89 | 84 | 78 | 72 |
| Low | 50 | 53 | 57 | 62 | 68 | 73 | 76 | 76 | 74 | 68 | 60 | 54 |

## Florida Keys

The Florida Keys lie just south of Florida's southern tip. This chain of about 3,000 small islands stretches more than 150 miles (241 km). Many people visit the Florida Keys to swim, fish, and water-ski.

## Walt Disney World

Walt Disney World near Orlando is one of the world's major tourist attractions. Millions of tourists visit the entertainment complex every year. Walt Disney World includes resorts, theme parks, water parks, entertainment, hotels, restaurants, and unique shops.

## Busch Gardens

Wild animals of Africa roam through Busch Gardens in Tampa. It is home to more than 2,700 animals, including zebras, hippopotamuses, and ostriches. Busch Gardens offers adventure rides, shows, and educational programs.

# HISTORY AND GOVERNMENT

Juan Ponce de León led the first European expedition to Florida.

Thousands of American Indians once lived in Florida. The Apalachee and Timucuan people lived in the north. The Atlantic coast was home to the Calusa. Other coastal groups included the Tequesta and Ais. Creek Indians moved in from Georgia and Alabama in the 1700s. Juan Ponce de León of Spain was the first European to reach Florida. He landed on the East Coast in 1513. Spain, France, and England fought over Florida for more than 200 years. The United States wanted it too. By 1821 Florida was a U.S. territory. It became the 27th state in 1845.

Florida's state government has three branches. The governor leads the executive branch. The legislature is made up of the 40-member Senate and the 120-member House of Representatives. They make Florida's laws. Florida's judges and courts are the judicial branch. They uphold the laws.

Florida's old capitol building now serves as a museum. The new capitol is located directly behind it.

# INDUSTRY

Florida is one of the world's top vacation spots. Tourism is Florida's largest industry, bringing millions of people to the state each year. Service industries make up about 90 percent of Florida's jobs. Service workers work in hotels, restaurants, and shops.

Farmland covers about 25 percent of Florida's land. Florida is a major world producer of citrus fruits and juices. One-third of the world's grapefruits come from the state. Florida has a strong fishing industry, while animal farms are a smaller part of Florida's agriculture.

Fishing is one of the state's most popular watersports.

A large part of Florida's economy is based on technology. In the 1950s the U.S. space program began at Cape Canaveral. In 1981 the personal computer was invented in Boca Raton. Today Florida companies make computer parts and communications equipment.

The beaches in Fort Lauderdale attract many tourists each year.

# POPULATION

The people of Florida have roots in many lands. Most Floridians have European ancestors. Long ago they came to Florida from England, Greece, Spain, and other nations. About one of every five Floridians is Hispanic. Their ancestors came from Spanish-speaking countries. Today many of Florida's Latinos are Cuban or Haitian. Around 3 million Floridians are African-American. About 2 percent are Asian. Only a small number of American Indians live in Florida today. They make up less than 1 percent of the state's population. Most of them live on the Seminole or Miccosukee reservations.

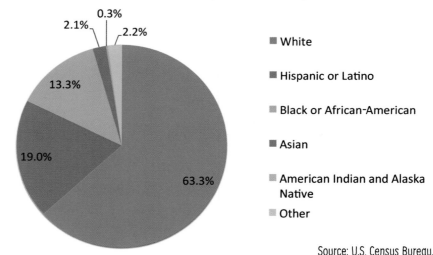

**Population by Ethnicity**

- 0.3%
- 2.1%
- 2.2%
- 13.3%
- 19.0%
- 63.3%

■ White

■ Hispanic or Latino

■ Black or African-American

■ Asian

■ American Indian and Alaska Native

■ Other

Source: U.S. Census Bureau.

The mascots of Florida State University represent the historical leader of the Seminole tribe.

# FAMOUS PEOPLE

**Juan Ponce de León** (1460–1521) was a Spanish explorer and the first European to reach Florida, arriving in 1513. He also gave Florida its name. He was born in Spain and lived in Puerto Rico.

**Janet Reno** (1938– ) was the first female U.S. attorney general. She served under President Bill Clinton from 1993 to 2001. Before that she was state attorney for Florida's Dade County. She was born in Miami.

**Chris Evert** (1954– ) won more than 150 tennis tournaments in the 1970s and 1980s. She earned a place in the Tennis Hall of Fame in 1995. She was born in Fort Lauderdale.

**Zora Neale Hurston** (1903–1960) wrote books about the culture and folklore of African-Americans in the South. She was raised in Eatonville.

**James Weldon Johnson** (1871–1938) wrote "Lift Every Voice and Sing." It's called the African-American national anthem. He served as the U.S. consul in Venezuela and Nicaragua. He was born in Jacksonville.

**Steve Carlton** (1944– ) was a star pitcher for the Philadelphia Phillies baseball team. He helped the team win the 1980 World Series. He was born in Miami.

# STATE SYMBOLS

Tree

sabal palm

Flower

orange blossom

Bird

mockingbird

Reptile

alligator

PebbleGo Next Bonus! To make a snack using Florida's citrus juices, go to www.pebblegonext.com and search keywords: **FL RECIPE**

## Marine Animal

manatee

## Butterfly

zebra longwing

## Freshwater Fish

largemouth bass

## Stone

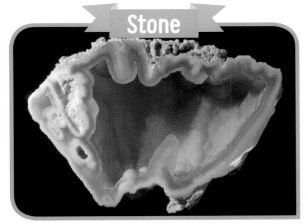

agatized coral

## Saltwater Fish

sailfish

## Gem

moonstone

21

# FAST FACTS

**STATEHOOD**
1845

**CAPITAL** ☆
Tallahassee

**LARGEST CITY** •
Jacksonville

**SIZE**
53,625 square miles (138,888 square kilometers)
land area (2010 U.S. Census Bureau)

**POPULATION**
19,552,860 (2013 U.S. Census estimate)

**STATE NICKNAME**
The Sunshine State

**STATE MOTTO**
"In God We Trust"

PebbleGo Next Bonus!
To learn the lyrics to
the state song, go to
www.pebblegonext.com
and search keywords:

**FL SONG**

# STATE SEAL

Florida's state seal shows a Seminole woman scattering flowers. In the background are a steamboat, a palm tree, and the sun. A gold circle wraps around the seal. The words "Great Seal of the State of Florida" circle the top of the seal. The words "In God We Trust" circle the bottom.

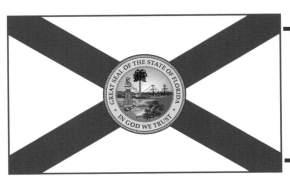

**PebbleGo Next Bonus!**
**To print and color**
**your own flag, go to**
**www.pebblegonext.com**
**and search keywords:**

**FL FLAG**

# STATE FLAG

Florida's state flag shows a red "X" on a plain white background. In the center is the state seal, which has symbols of the state's history, industry, and wildlife. The seal shows a Seminole woman scattering flowers, a steamboat, and a sabal palm tree, which is the state tree. Rays of the rising sun stream in the background.

## MINING PRODUCTS

phosphate rock, limestone, portland cement, petroleum, sand and gravel

## MANUFACTURED GOODS

computer and electronic equipment, food products, chemicals, machinery, paper, plastics and rubber products

## FARM PRODUCTS

oranges, grapefruits, sugarcane, beef cattle, vegetables, greenhouse plants, dairy products

## PROFESSIONAL SPORTS TEAMS

Florida Bobcats (AFL)
Orlando Predators (AFL)
Tampa Bay Storm (AFL)
Florida Marlins (MLB)
Tampa Bay Devil Rays (MLB)
Miami Fusion (MLS)
Tampa Bay Mutiny (MLS)
Miami Heat (NBA)
Orlando Magic (NBA)
Miami Sol (WNBA)
Orlando Miracle (WNBA)
Jacksonville Jaguars (NFL)
Miami Dolphins (NFL)
Tampa Bay Buccaneers (NFL)
Florida Panthers (NHL)
Tampa Bay Lightning (NHL)

# FLORIDA TIMELINE

**1513** Spanish explorer Juan Ponce de León reaches Florida and claims it for Spain.

**1565** The Spanish found St. Augustine in northern Florida. It is the first permanent European settlement in what is now the United States.

**1620** The Pilgrims establish a colony in the New World in present-day Massachusetts.

**1763** Spain gives Florida to Great Britain in exchange for Havana, Cuba.

## 1775–1783

American colonists fight for their independence from Great Britain in the Revolutionary War.

## 1783

Spanish forces regain control of Florida from Great Britain, whose troops were weakened by the Revolutionary War.

## 1817–1818

U.S. General Andrew Jackson and his troops look for runaway slaves and clash with Seminole Indians, who are protecting the runaways. Jackson's raid starts the First Seminole War (1817–1818). The Second Seminole War is fought from 1835 to 1842. The Third Seminole War is fought from 1855 to 1858. The Seminoles are forced to move west.

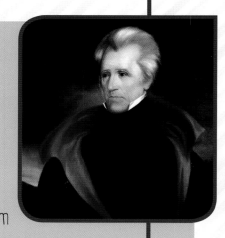

## 1822

U.S. Congress establishes the Territory of Florida.

**1845** — Florida becomes the 27th state on March 3.

**1861** — Florida leaves the United States to join a new country called the Confederate States of America.

**1861–1865** — The Union and the Confederacy fight the Civil War. Florida fights for the Confederacy. Florida supplies salt and cattle to the Confederate Army.

**1868** — Florida rejoins the United States.

**1914–1918** — World War I is fought; the United States enters the war in 1917.

**1926**

Florida's high land prices fall, causing the state's economy to crash.

**1939–1945**

World War II is fought; the United States enters the war in 1941.

**1969**

*Apollo 11* is launched from NASA's Kennedy Space Center on Florida's Atlantic coast. It is the first spacecraft to land astronauts on the moon.

**1971**

Walt Disney World opens near Orlando.

**1992**

Hurricane Andrew hits southern Florida, causing about $25 billion in property damage.

**2000**

After recounts and a Supreme Court ruling, Texas Governor George W. Bush wins Florida's electoral votes, winning the U.S. presidential election over Vice President Al Gore.

**2011**

The space shuttle *Atlantis* lands at Kennedy Space Center on Florida's Atlantic coast, ending the space shuttle program that began in 1981.

**2015**

Scientists at the Scripps Research Institute in Jupiter, Florida, design a molecule that may work in an HIV vaccine.

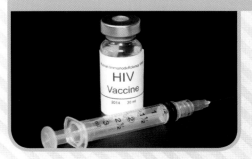

# Glossary

**ancestor** *(AN-ses-tuhr)*—a family member who lived a long time ago

**clash** *(KLASH)*—to fight or argue

**consul** *(KON-suhl)*—someone appointed by the government of a country to live and work in another country; his or her job is to protect fellow citizens who are working or traveling abroad

**culture** *(KUHL-chuhr)*—a people's way of life, ideas, art, customs, and traditions

**executive** *(ig-ZE-kyuh-tiv)*—the branch of government that makes sure laws are followed

**folklore** *(FOHK-lor)*—tales, sayings, and customs among a group of people

**industry** *(IN-duh-stree)*—a business which produces a product or provides a service

**legislature** *(LEJ-iss-lay-chur)*—a group of elected officials who have the power to make or change laws for a country or state

**peninsula** *(puh-NIN-suh-luh)*—a piece of land surrounded by water on three sides

**permanent** *(PUR-muh-nuhnt)*—lasting for a long time or forever

**unique** *(yoo-NEEK)*—one of a kind

# Read More

**Ganeri, Anita.** *United States of America: A Benjamin Blog and His Inquisitive Dog Guide.* Country Guides. Chicago: Heinemann Raintree, 2015.

**Hess, Debra.** *Florida.* It's My State! New York: Cavendish Square Publishing, 2014.

**Meinking, Mary.** *What's Great About Florida?* Our Great States. Minneapolis: Lerner Publications, 2015.

# Internet Sites

FactHound offers a safe, fun way to find Internet sites related to this book. All of the sites on FactHound have been researched by our staff.

Here's all you do:

Visit *www.facthound.com*

Type in this code: 9781515703952

Check out projects, games and lots more at
**www.capstonekids.com**

# Critical Thinking Using the Common Core

1. Most of Florida is a peninsula. What does this mean? (Craft and Structure)

2. Florida is one of the world's top vacation spots. What are some of its major attractions? (Key Ideas and Details)

3. If you could travel anywhere in Florida, where would you go? Why? (Integration of Knowledge and Ideas)

# Index